BEACH SAFETY

Dr. Peter R. Chambers
Illustrated by Gal Weizman

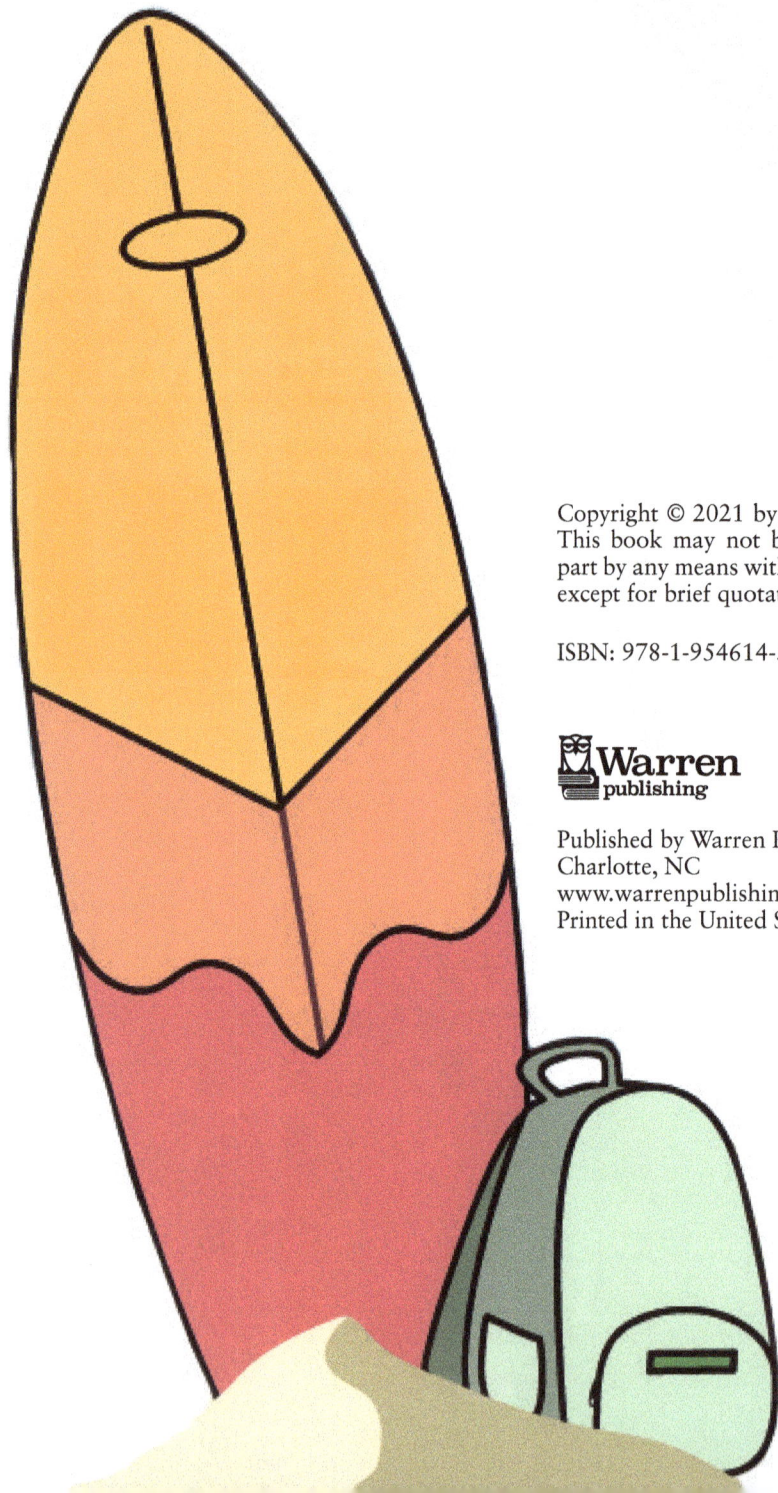

ISBN: 978-1-954614-33-8

Warren
publishing

Published by Warren Publishing
Charlotte, NC
www.warrenpublishing.net
Printed in the United States

To my surfer girl, Tricia,
who I watched on the shore.
In the lineup together,
day in and day out.

Swimming at the beach can be great fun.
There are so many things to see and do,

but it's important to remember how to be safe whether you're on the shore or in the water.

Before you go to the beach, there are a few things you should do to make sure you are safe.

First, do you know how to swim?
If you don't, you should take swim lessons. Swim lessons teach you how to move around in the water safely. You'll learn how to float on your back and how to keep your head above water.

NO RUNNING

You should also be sure that you learn CPR. CPR is a life-saving action and you are never too young to learn. You'll be able to help others around you in an emergency if you know how to do chest compressions and rescue breathing.

Once you arrive at the beach, there are actions you can take and things you should know that will help you stay safe whether you're building sand castles on the beach or surfing an ocean wave.

First and most importantly, you should swim near a lifeguard. Lifeguards are the men and women trained as first responders on the beach. They do all sorts of jobs, including watching you when you're in, on, and around the ocean and preventing accidents from happening.

✔ LIFE JACKET
✔ SUNSCREEN
✔ FIRST AID KIT
✔ DRINKING WATER
✔ SWIM WITH A BUDDY
✔ HAVE A WATER WATCHER

Next, you should be sure you are wearing sunscreen.
No one likes a sunburn, so be sure you slather sunscreen on
your arms, legs, face, neck and ears several times during the day.

You should also know what the meaning is for each of the flags that fly when you are at the beach. There are five different flags.

Green means safe to swim, calm conditions

Yellow means caution, medium hazard

Single Red means dangerous conditions high hazard

Double Red means very dangerous water is closed

Purple means caution dangerous marine life

When you are swimming at the beach, you should be aware of who is around you and what is going on near you. Be watchful.

And, you should swim as a pair. This means you should not go in the water alone, but you should swim with a family member, friend, or swimming buddy. You can keep your eyes on them and they can keep their eyes on YOU!

Also, while at the beach swimming, be sure to watch out for marine life. The ocean is their home, so keep your eyes open for jellyfish, stingrays, tortoises, and even sharks.

It's also important to not swim by a pier or the jetties. These are areas where platforms are supported by tall pillars of wood in the water. The water near these areas is rough and choppy and the bottom can shift quickly.

Staying safe while swimming at the beach also means knowing what a rip current is. A rip current is a channel of water traveling out to deeper water faster than the rest of the water, and they happen often at the beach. If you end up in a rip current while swimming, don't panic! Call for help and swim parallel to the shore until you can leave the water.

If you remember these tips, swimming in open water, like the beach, can be a great time for you and your friends and family.

NORTH MYRTLE BEACH LIFEGUARD FOUNDATION

www.nmblf.org

ACKNOWLEDGMENTS

Thank you to the following for their commitment to beach safety:
- The Department of Ocean Rescue North Myrtle Beach Public Safety.
- The United States Lifesaving Association (USLA) leadership-past, present, and future.

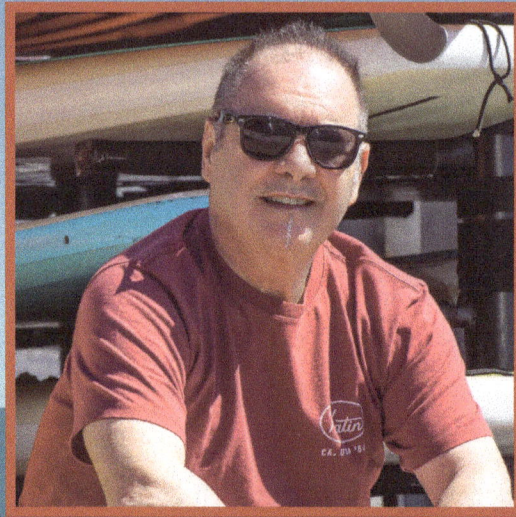

PETER R. CHAMBERS, PHD, DO
a.k.a. "Surf Doc"

When not in the water, Dr. Chambers is an emergency room physician. He is an open water lifeguard and serves as the medical director with the North Myrtle Beach Ocean Rescue in North Myrtle Beach, South Carolina. He is a true waterman, and a proud United States Air Force Veteran/Flight Surgeon.

Surf Doc's motto is to always
"SWIM NEAR A LIFEGUARD."